D1130599

George Washington Carver

A LIFE OF DEVOTION

by Robin Nelson

PULL AHEAD BOOKS
Biographies

Lerner Publications Company • Minneapolis

Photo Acknowledgments

The images in this book are used with the permission of: Comstock Images, p. 4; George Washington Carver National Monument, p. 6; Library of Congress, pp. 8 (LC-USZ62-117666), 9 (LC-USZ62-78481), 12 (LC-J601-302), 14 (LC-USZ62-49568), 15 (LC-USZ62-2248), 18 (LC-USZ62-114302), 25 (LC-USW38-000165-D); Courtesy of the Simpson College Archives, pp. 10, 11; National Cotton Council, p. 16; Tuskegee University, pp. 17, 21, 22; © Brown Brothers, pp. 20, 24, 27; © Envision/CORBIS, p. 23; USDA Photo, p. 26. Front cover: © Hulton Archive/Getty Images.

Lerner Publications Company
A division of Lerner Publishing Group
241 First Avenue North
Minneapolis, MN 55401 U.S.A.

Website address: www.lernerbooks.com

Words in **bold type** are explained in a glossary on page 31.

Library of Congress Cataloging-in-Publication Data

Nelson, Robin.
      George Washington Carver : a life of devotion / by Robin Nelson.
        p.   cm. – (Pull ahead books)
      Includes index.
      ISBN-13: 978-0-8225-6461-4 (lib. bdg. : alk. paper)
      ISBN-10: 0-8225-6461-0 (lib. bdg. : alk. paper)
      1. Carver, George Washington, 1864?-1943–Juvenile literature. 2. African American agriculturists–Biography–Juvenile literature. 3. Agriculturists–United States–Biography–Juvenile literature. I. Title.
      S417.C3N45 2007
      630.92--dc22   2006021942

Manufactured in the United States of America
1 2 3 4 5 6 – JR – 12 11 10 09 08 07

Table of Contents

Devoted to Helping

Do you know how peanuts can help farmers? George Washington Carver did. George Washington Carver was a scientist. He was **devoted** to helping people with their farms. He spent his life teaching people how to take care of plants and soil.

George explored these woods.

Devoted to Nature

George loved nature. As a child, he walked through the woods collecting rocks and plants. He began to help neighbors and friends with sick plants. They gave him the nickname "the plant doctor."

George's school had only African-American students.

George went to a school for African-American children.

At that time, white children and black children did not go to the same schools.

Students learn about cotton at this school for black children.

George studied at Simpson College and Iowa State Agricultural College.

George was devoted to learning. In those days, not many African Americans went to **college**. But George did.

George *(far right)* sits with other college students.

In college, George studied plant and farm science. He learned how to make **soil** better for plants.

Devoted to Teaching

After college, George taught other college students about plants and soil. He was the first black teacher at his college.

Booker T. Washington

One day, George received a letter from a man named Booker T. Washington. Booker started a college for African Americans.

All the teachers and students at his college were African Americans. Booker wanted George to teach at his college. George agreed.

George teaches a class

Many farmers grew cotton near the college. But the cotton plants were taking **nutrients** out of the soil.

A cotton plant

George works with one of his students.

The plants could not grow without these nutrients. George taught his students how to make soil get better.

George wanted to help farmers make the soil better.

Devoted to Peanuts

George knew that growing peanuts could help the soil in the South. He said that for one year farmers should plant peanuts instead of cotton. The peanuts would put nutrients back into the soil. Farmers could plant cotton the next year. Each year, farmers would switch plants. This is called **crop rotation**.

But this caused another problem for farmers. What could they do with the peanuts they grew?

A woman stands in a peanut field.

George talks about how farmers could use the peanuts they grew.

George was devoted to helping the farmers with this problem. He began to study peanuts.

George does experiments with peanuts.

George found more than 300 things
that could be made with peanuts!

Peanut brittle was one of the many products George created.

He made paint, soap, medicine, paper, and glue from peanuts.

George became famous for his work with farmers and peanuts.

President Franklin D. Roosevelt congratulated George on his work with peanuts.

He gave speeches all over the United
States about peanuts and farming.

George Washington Carver was a great scientist.

George did many kinds of experiments in his laboratory.

He devoted his life to science, plants, and farming. George helped farmers grow better crops.

GEORGE WASHINGTON CARVER TIMELINE

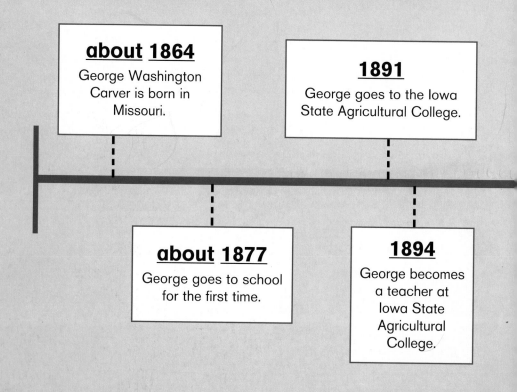

about 1864

George Washington Carver is born in Missouri.

1891

George goes to the Iowa State Agricultural College.

about 1877

George goes to school for the first time.

1894

George becomes a teacher at Iowa State Agricultural College.

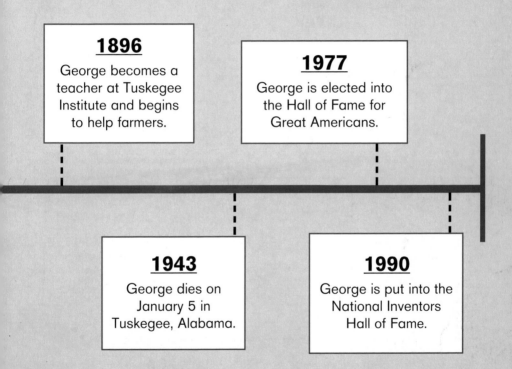

1896
George becomes a teacher at Tuskegee Institute and begins to help farmers.

1977
George is elected into the Hall of Fame for Great Americans.

1943
George dies on January 5 in Tuskegee, Alabama.

1990
George is put into the National Inventors Hall of Fame.

More about George Washington Carver

- George was born a slave. When his parents died, he was set free and raised by his former owners.

- George loved flowers. He wore a fresh flower on his jacket every day.

- George created over 300 things from peanuts, but he did not invent peanut butter.

Websites

George Washington Carver Coloring and Activity Book
http://www.usda.gov/oo/colorbook.htm

George Washington Carver National Monument
http://www.nps.gov/gwca

The Legacy of George Washington Carver
http://www.lib.iastate.edu/spcl/gwc/home.html

Glossary

college: a school some people go to after high school

crop rotation: planting different plants on the same land to improve the soil

devoted: giving time and attention to something

nutrients: something in soil that helps plants grow

soil: the top part of the ground

Index